RETAIL ARBITRAGE 101

BY:

JOHN NAVARRO

TABLE OF CONTENTS

What is Retail Arbitrage?

Retail Arbitrage is the process of buying something at a lower price point to instantly resell it at a higher price point.

Obviously, with Retail Arbitrage the arbitrage part of it is not as instantaneous as one who has traded in the markets might mistake that part of the term for.

While a perfect Retail Arbitrage can be quick and easy, this is not a get rich-quick scheme; it takes hard work and dedication to build an online business and in Retail Arbitrage 101, you are going to learn everything you need to survive and thrive on the internet.

You are going to learn some of the top secrets that the gurus who teach Retail Arbitrage do not share! Notice, that you are only taught one end of the spectrum, either Amazon or Ebay, here you will learn the foundations to sell on both marketplaces.

The best in the business follow the trends and capitalize off of them.

Also included as a bonus at the end of the book is the Retail Arbitrage list; this list contains places you can go right now and utilize Retail Arbitrage!

Positioning Your Retail Arbitrage for Maximum Profitability

This step is one of the **most coveted** secrets in the Retail Arbitrage community. I have never seen this information shared anywhere else. It is how the top Retail Arbitragers are able to buy items at higher prices and still resell them below their competition. This trick is known as *stacking savings*.

If you want to stack savings, it starts before you even go to the store. Research your Retail Arbitrage route or stores you plan to visit and check online for any coupons that you can use. Coupons go a long way in Retail Arbitrage, and it makes a huge difference when your competitor is buying the same item you are, but you have a 25% off coupon for it.

That puts you in a better position to profit and be more competitive in the very beginning. You do not have to worry about differentiating yourself from the competitor, because you have the superior price. They are forced with the task of differentiating themselves from you! The best thing is that if you are in a niche selling an item with little to no competition any additional savings at the register is like money in your pocket! Some stores give out coupons for up to 40% off; these coupons are often times good on clearance or heavily marked down items! Not all of these coupons are advertised and it pays to do your research before you go to the store or online to purchase! Even an extra 5% is 5% more in your pocket instantly!

The next step is to utilize a cash-back card. PayPal offers a debit card with Cashback and this is a great way for you to utilize an extra percent on all purchases without having to have credit/debt looming over your head. Use this card on every Retail Arbitrage purchase, because that extra percent off does add up at the end of the year. Some credit cards offer up to 5% cashback at certain locations or during specific promotional periods, so this all can be used to stack savings.

If you are making an online purchase, check a site like Ebates or Fatwallet before making your purchase, to get even more cashback!

Featured Stores

carter's	6.0% Cash Back!
PC. RICHARD&Son	3.0% Cash Back!
J.CREW FACTORY	3.0% Cash Back!
Walmart Save money. Live better.	2.0% Cash Back!
kmart	6.0% Cash Back!
AMERICAN EAGLE OUTFITTERS ac.com	4.0% Cash Back!
(Home Depot)	4.0% Cash Back!
Hotels.com	4.25% Cash Back!
Dell Small Business	4.0% Cash Back!
Neiman Marcus lastcall	5.0% Cash Back!
JoS. A. BANK	8.0% Cash Back!
NORDSTROM	6.0% Cash Back!

See all Online Stores

Featured Coupons

Overstock.com
10% off your purchase!
Plus 2.5% Cash Back!

DSW
Womens Sandals. $29.95 and under.
Plus 4.0% Cash Back!

Best Buy
See this Week's HP Printers on Sale!
Plus 1.0% Cash Back!

Folica Beauty Supply
Get 15% off orders of $30+, 20% off orders of $60+ and 25% off orders of $90+.
CODE: SHOPPING
Plus 4.0% Cash Back!

1800CONTACTS
New customers save $30 off $150!
Plus 5.0% Cash Back!

AT&T
U-family TV and Elite Internet (6 Mbps) with $200 in Rewards Cards Now: $49 per month.
Plus Up to $55.00 Cash Back!

Stage Stores
25% Site-wide on your favorite brands at Bealls, Goodys, Peebles, Palais Royal and Stage!
Plus 3.0% Cash Back!

Old Navy
New Cropped Pants Sale Was: $29.94 Now: $19.
Plus 2.0% Cash Back!

Adam & Eve
Get 25% off one item only!
CODE: EBATES25
Plus 10.0% Cash Back!

Amazon Local
$5 off any purchase for new customers!
Code can only be applied once per user.
CODE: Ebates14
Plus 3.0% Cash Back!

Taking your savings to the next level

You now know how to stack your savings, which some of the most seasoned Retail Arbitragers lack the knowledge to do. It's time to take it to the next level. This next step is a very little known secret in the Retail Arbitrage community, and the gurus who offer paid lessons / guides, do not share it. You can take your stacked savings to the next level by combining them with discounted gift cards!

That's right not only do some retail stores and outlets offer up to 40% off with coupons and you can stack these savings with additional cash back offers, but you can also purchase discounted gift cards to save up to another 5% to 40%!

A lot of times you are able to purchase these cards and a lot of times instantly get them printed out for immediate use in the stores!

There are two great places to get discounted gift cards safely and securely. One curates all of the discounted gift cards from the internet and displays them in a sortable format. So this one is currently utilized to find the best deals on discounted gift cards, it is called GiftCardFrom.com.

The second website delivers most orders electronically and you are able to easily print off the gift cards for instant use within the retail store / outlet, it is called Gift Card Zen. Between these two websites it is easy to find discounted gift cards for not only retail stores, but gas stations, and on food, we get hungry out there!

Follow the trend and profit

As was stated in the intro, the best in the business follow the trends.

The trends are not just limited to toys; many people have capitalized off of geographical specific merchandise such as local sport team's jerseys, or other sports memorabilia that may be available at one Wal-Mart in Texas, but not the one in Alaska. I have even purchased sports themed lighters and successfully resold them at a premium.

Do you remember the Duck Dynasty show?

At the height of the show, people were making over a 500% return on items purchased and resold, after expenses were taken out.

People were purchasing Duck Dynasty T-shirts for as little as $1.00 without any coupons or extra savings and reselling them for upwards of $20.00 each!

It doesn't stop there, pretty much anything that is popular will go through a series of price reduction and when it does you need to be ready to capitalize on it.

Some of the best Retail Arbitragers often buy trending Legos (think specific Legos themes centered on another topic) on clearance and resell them for up to 10x their purchase price. Not only that, but regular sets of Legos can be purchased on clearance and resold at the same premium. It's all about finding the right set with a good amount of pieces for a good deal.

One determined Retail Arbitrager with help from his wife made $6,000 in 3 days from buying and reselling this very Lego set. The hardest challenge that was faced by the couple was sourcing the product sustainably. Like all great Retail Arbitrages, it can only last for so long and all supplies do eventually run dry, but $6,000 in 3 days is a fantastic and noteworthy Retail Arbitrage.

A "Frozen" Themed Playset that was bought in stores for
$119.99, was selling online for an average of $250.00.
This was a quick and easy sell for a lot of Retail
Arbitragers who were following the Frozen trend. People
are still making money off of Frozen goods they purchased
when it was first released.

One of the most famous Retail Arbitrages ever was the Tickle Me Elmo craze. This fad would lead to this $28.00 Elmo being sold for up to $7,100 by someone in Denver. I was able to get my hands on two.

A Quick Review

If you only remember two things from what you have
read so far it should be:

1.   Follow the trend.
2.   Find merchandise that is heavily marked down or
on clearance.

Finding opportunities in markdowns and clearance

We have learned that if you want to be successful in Retail Arbitrage, you need to **follow the trends** and **find merchandise that is heavily marked down or on clearance**. However, sometimes it can be difficult to differentiate from all of the items on clearance.

How can you tell which products are the profitable ones, which ones are worth taking a risk on, and which ones you want to avoid?

The easiest way is to research each product you come across on your own. There are some scanning apps and other apps available for purchase that can streamline the process, but be wary sometimes not all of the information is accurate and furthermore there are stories of Retail Arbitragers being kicked out of places like Target for scanning products.

That is why I recommend doing it the old fashioned way, it may take a little longer, but you are able to get more accurate data for your research.

If it has a major UPC or EAN number, you can enter that into Amazon's search engine and see if it is being sold there. If it is being sold there, you can see the number of sellers selling the product as well as how much they are selling it for.

After you get an idea of the product from Amazon, take the title (or parts of it if you are unable to search it the first time successfully) and enter it into the Ebay.com search and check the competition as well as see how much the product is selling for there. You can try to use the UPC or EAN number, but this is not always successful on EBay.

Now that you know what the product is selling for, if you think you see an opportunity, you need to do some basic calculations to make sure you can actually make a decent return on investment. You do not want to buy a product that is selling online for $30.00 for $10.00 and it costs $9 to ship. **That is not a worthwhile Retail Arbitrage.**

More Examples of Retail Arbitrage

We will start with Supreme NYC, this is a popular brand of clothing that yields a high profit with retail arbitrage.

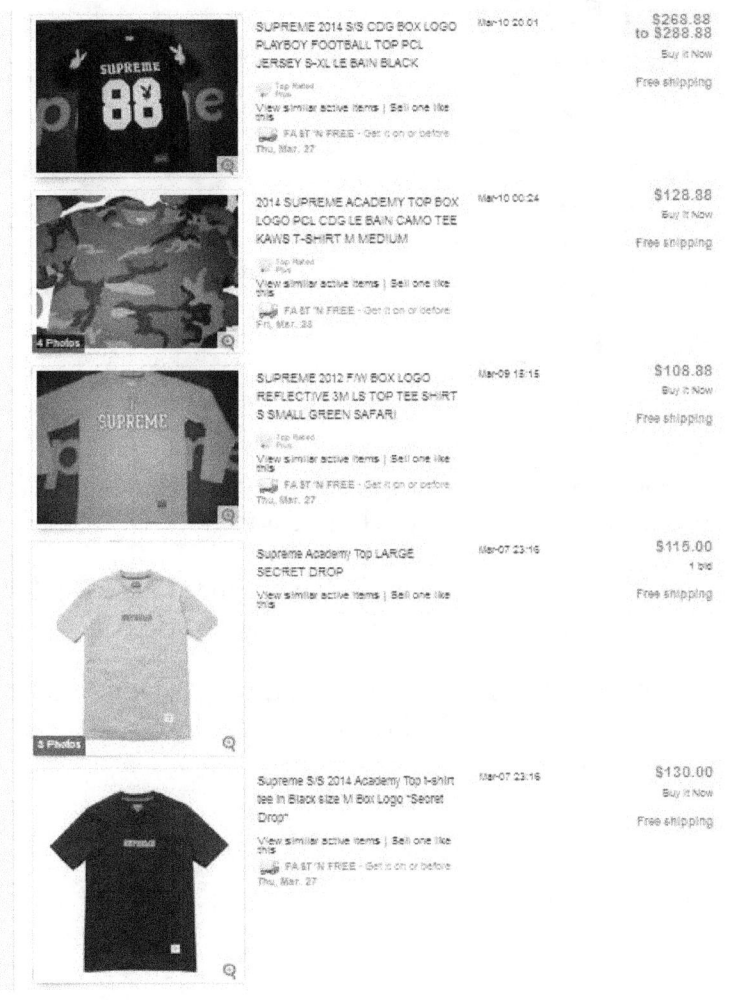

As you can see the T shirts (tops) sell for all price ranges.

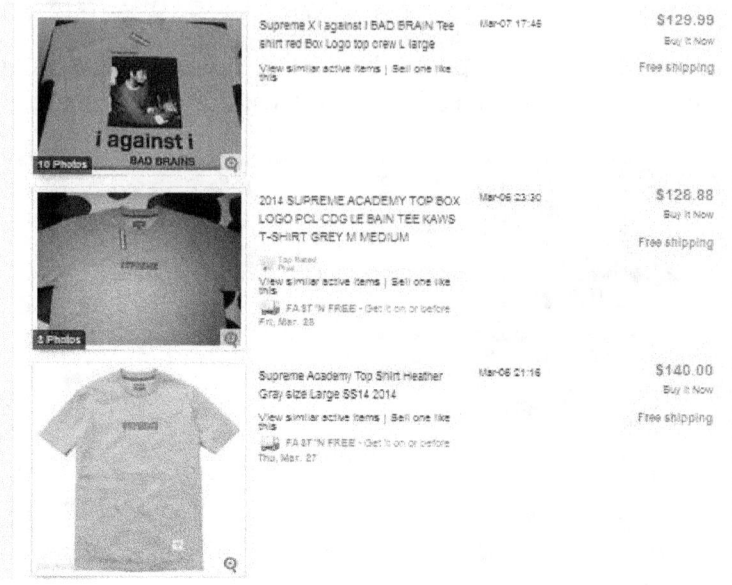

These are just a few of thousands of listings that have successfully sold.

Most of these t shirts can be bought for around $68.00 RETAIL. (Think before any additional stacked savings).

Supreme is a very popular brand and with that being said, it is highly profitable.

Other Examples of Retail Arbitrage

Gymboree is a popular baby and toddler clothing brand.

Gymboree is sought after by moms worldwide!

As you can see these are just simple tops being sold, that can be found in the store for as low as $2.00 - $3.00, depending on the sale and season.

NWT Gymboree Mr. Magician Size 5T White 3 Magicians Moustache Top Shirt
Top Rated Plus
View similar active items | Sell one like this
Mar-21 21:11
$12.00
Buy It Now

NWT Gymboree Camp Yosemite Size 5T Green Jeep Let's Go Camping Shirt Top
Top Rated Plus
View similar active items | Sell one like this
Mar-21 21:11
$14.00
Buy It Now

NWT Gymboree Fox Trail Long Sleeve Tops/Tees/Body suit-12-18/18-24 Mo 2T 3T 4T 5T
Top Rated Plus
View similar active items | Sell one like this
FAST 'N FREE - Get it on or before Wed, Mar. 29
Mar-20 20:20
$12.00 to $14.50
Buy It Now
Free shipping

NWT Gymboree Shark Patrol Size 5T White Ringer Tee Plaid Shark Shirt Top
Top Rated Plus
View similar active items | Sell one like this
Mar-20 17:07
$12.50
Buy It Now

NWT Boy's Gymboree dog pelican tank top shirts ~ 5T
Top Rated Plus
View similar active items | Sell one like this
Mar-20 01:55
$12.50
Buy It Now

GIRLS 4T OR 5T GYMBOREE SNAIL SMOCKED TOP SHIRT FAIRY GARDEN NWT FREE SHIPPING	Mar-22 23:30	$13.99
		Buy It Now
		Free shipping
View similar active items | Sell one like this		
NWT Gymboree Woodland Friends Baby Toddler Girl Clothes Top Brown 12m 4T 5T	Mar-22 18:49	$13.99
		Buy It Now
		Free shipping
View similar active items | Sell one like this		
Expedited shipping available		
NWT Gymboree Growing Flowers Snail 2T Top Shirt Blouse	Mar-22 12:02	$12.99
		Buy It Now
		Free shipping
Top Rated Plus		
View similar active items | Sell one like this		
FAST 'N FREE - Get it on or before Thu, Mar. 27		
GYMBOREE 2T NWT "Equestrian Club" Tunic Top Blouse * Pretty Floral Embroidery	Mar-22 08:01	$12.00
		Buy It Now
		Free shipping
View similar active items | Sell one like this		
FAST 'N FREE - Get it on or before Fri, Mar. 28		

We have now seen two simple examples of retail arbitrage, but there are more methods that can be utilized to help you get more profit from your arbitrage.

See the example below.

Retail Arbitrage Twists

The **main point and example** of this arbitrage is the combining of other brands to get the most money for lower quality brands. For example in these clothing lots, there are popular brands such as Gymboree and Baby Gap; however there are less popular brands such as Cherokee and maybe non branded items as well. Always think outside the box and try new things to make profit!

They will all sell for the same per piece by being bundled this way.

18 Pc Lot BABY GIRLS WONDERKIDS TANK TOPS shorts New 12 MONTHS Summer Clothes
View similar active items | Sell one like this
Mar-09 12:21
$49.99
1 bid

Lot Of Girl's Infant's Toddler 2T 24 M Shirts Tops Shorts Clothes New With Tags
View similar active items | Sell one like this
Mar-02 19:10
$20.99
1 bid

Lot Of Girl's Infant's Size 18 Months Shirts Tops Shorts Clothes New With Tags
View similar active items | Sell one like this
Mar-02 18:42
$15.50
2 bids

Lot Of Girl's Infant's Size 12-24 Months Shirts Clothes Tops New With Tags
View similar active items | Sell one like this
Mar-02 18:33
$21.51
10 bids

In this arbitrage method, auctions are being used to get the quickest "cash flow" and "short-term exposure", which may lead to a lower overall selling price, but possibly more volume being sold. It is a position that has to be evaluated and tweaked to meet the needs of you and your business.

This method works for more than just baby and toddler clothing.

Researching on Ebay

So you found a potential retail arbitrage and you want to know how to either make the most out of it or sell it the quickest?

Let's first start with maximizing profits.

So starting at the Ebay home page, we type in a somewhat broad description of the item we are looking to learn more about, in this case it is a t shirt, so we want to see similar variations and colors that may have sold too, to get an overall idea of that particular shirt's appeal and selling prices.

First we will look at live active selling listings.

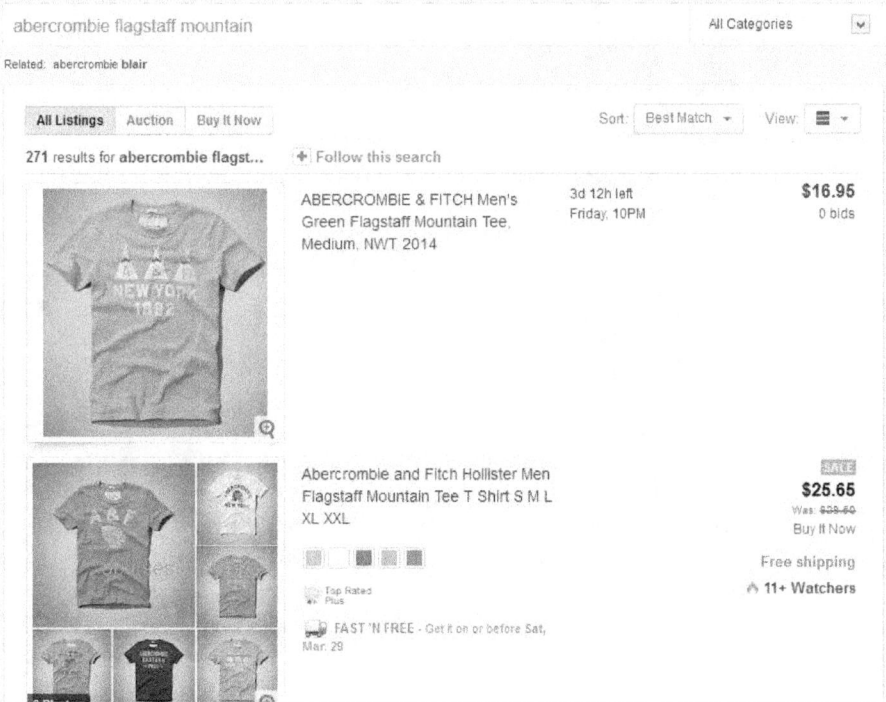

Remember we are looking over all of the different variations to get a broad idea of how it performs.

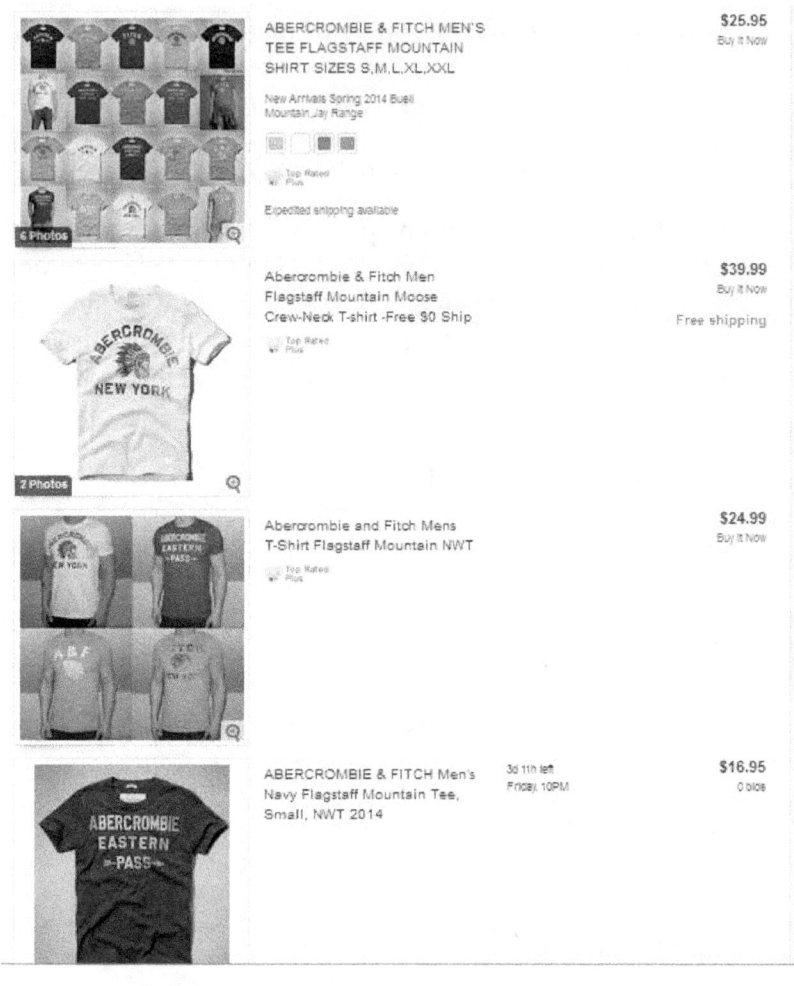

Next, click on one of the top 5 in the best match, preferably top 3, but sometimes a new listing or two will be there for a moment while it cycles through.

Abercrombie and Fitch Hollister Men Flagstaff Mountain Tee T

Item condition:	New with tags
Color	- Select - ⌄
Size (Men's):	- Select - ⌄
Quantity:	1 More than 10 available / 105 sold
Was:	US $28.50
You save:	$2.85 (10%) Sale ends in 7 days
Price:	US $25.65

Buy It Now

Add to cart

126 watchers   Add to watch list ⌄

★ Add to collection

Experienced Seller	Free Shipping	105 Sold

New customers get $10 back on 1st purchase
Subject to credit approval. See terms

Shipping   FREE Standard Shipping | See details

So, it appears the shirt may be somewhat popular considering one of the top listings has **105 sold**, but we need to see in what time they have sold and which particular variations to get a better idea.

Click on the **X amount sold link** for example this one is 105 sold. You will see something similar to what you see below, depending on the seller's settings.

User ID	Variation	Price	Quantity	Date of
private listing – buyers' identities protected	Color: Red Size (Men's): XL	US $25.65	1	Mar-25
private listing – buyers' identities protected	Color: Red Size (Men's): 2XL	US $25.65	1	Mar-25
private listing – buyers' identities protected	Color: Green Size (Men's): XL	US $25.65	1	Mar-25
private listing – buyers' identities protected	Color: Navy Size (Men's): XL	US $25.65	1	Mar-25
private listing – buyers' identities protected	Color: White Size (Men's): M	US $25.65	1	Mar-25
private listing – buyers' identities protected	Color: Blue Size (Men's): M	US $25.65	1	Mar-24
private listing – buyers' identities protected	Color: Blue Size (Men's): M	US $25.65	1	Mar-24
private listing – buyers' identities protected	Color: White Size (Men's): L	US $25.65	1	Mar-24
private listing – buyers' identities protected	Color: Navy Size (Men's): L	US $25.65	1	Mar-24
private listing – buyers' identities protected	Color: Red Size (Men's): L	US $25.65	1	Mar-24
private listing – buyers' identities protected	Color: White Size (Men's): L	US $25.65	1	Mar-24
private listing – buyers' identities protected	Color: Red Size (Men's): L	US $25.65	1	Mar-24
private listing – buyers' identities protected	Color: Red Size (Men's): L	US $25.65	3	Mar-24
private listing – buyers' identities protected	Color: Gray Size (Men's): M	US $25.65	1	Mar-23
private listing – buyers' identities protected	Color: Green Size (Men's): M	US $25.65	1	Mar-23
private listing – buyers' identities protected	Color: Red	US $25.65	1	Mar-23

We can see this is a pretty popular listing, with multiple items selling a day and on top of that, sometimes multiple quantities. This is just a small amount of the total results, which shows green as a good average and red being the most popular here.

Let's take it a step further now and look at the sold listings, the problem with relying on sold listings is a lot of bigger variation listings will not be in here, because they are actively still selling, so I recommend using best match results always before sold.

NEW Abercrombie & Fitch Mens Flagstaff Mountain Premiun Embellished T-Shirt

Feb-17 11:44

$23.99
Buy It Now

Free shipping

Top Rated Plus

View similar active items | Sell one like this

FAST 'N FREE - Get it on or before Sat, Mar. 29

New NWT Abercrombie & Fitch Flagstaff Mountain T-Shirt Tee Men's Blue

Jan-18 09:55

$21.99
Buy It Now

Free shipping

View similar active items | Sell one like this

FAST 'N FREE - Get it on or before Mon, Mar. 31

ABERCROMBIE & FITCH White FLAGSTAFF MOUNTAIN Muscle T-Shirt MENS M MEDIUM NEW

Jan-09 05:19

$23.99
10 bids

Top Rated Plus

View similar active items | Sell one like this

One-day shipping available

Let's look at what methods we can use to get the "quickest" profit. To do so, we need to view the fixed price best match listings and auctions.

What you are ideally looking for is a recently ended auction or an auction that is 1-4 hours away from ending, so you can get an idea of the peak bidding. Also, please keep in mind the success of an auction is just like any other

Ebay listing, it depends on time started, time ended, pictures, title, description, shipping costs, and most importantly price!

ABERCROMBIE & FITCH Men's Green Flagstaff Mountain Tee, Medium, NWT 2014

3d 11h left
Friday, 10PM

$16.95
0 bids

ABERCROMBIE & FITCH Men's Navy Flagstaff Mountain Tee, Small, NWT 2014

3d 11h left
Friday, 10PM

$16.95
0 bids

ABERCROMBIE & FITCH Men's Green Flagstaff Mountain Tee, XL, NWT 2014

3d 11h left
Friday, 10PM

$16.95
0 bids

Sometimes you are not able to get the best auction results, either due to someone not actively selling it, or auctions just starting like above. From the starting price of the auction, it appears to be an organized sell, so maybe this seller is doing these types of auctions often, or maybe it is a one-time auction there is no way to be sure.

That is why it is best to use multiple fixed price listings, we already used one before, to get an idea of how the item sells and how often, now we will use another one to compare it against that price as well as trying to find the optimum salability price.

Looking at the example below, we will learn a lot more about the potential retail arbitrage.

We can see that 65 sold, so about **37% less sold** on this listing that the previous best match example.

Why could this be? Take note of the **higher price point**, and the **shipping cost** of $2.9.

The other listing was $0.30 cents cheaper, and had free standard shipping. The other listing (first best match example) has fewer variations, so it does not potentially have as much exposure as far as variations go, but it surpassed the second example listing using other methods to set itself apart and drive buyers.

These are all things to keep in mind, when you are researching the best price or salability of your retail arbitrage.

From the information we have seen, we can gather it is most likely best to make a fixed price listing with free shipping, priced at or around $24.99 **scheduled usually on Monday or Friday for maximum initial exposure.** The schedule works for most items and categories and can be used as a general rule on listing.

However, if you are a seller with a store, the best option would be to price the item for $26.99 and put it on sale for 5% off. This seems to give you a temporary boost in best match, as well as show up as a sale in other listings, as well as putting you as the current lowest price point. When using this method, be sure to keep an eye on your sale start and end dates, there is nothing worse than forgetting your sale ended and now you are the highest price point! When applied and monitored correctly, the **sale method** is a sure method!

More information on Retail Arbitrage

Some of the most profitable retail arbitrages take place in actual physical retail stores and outlets. The reason being is the inventory in these stores is not accessible or able to be purchased on the internet. Thus, it is often full of lower priced and more readily available items.

More often than not, the stores have lower prices than they do online, as well as more accessible inventory.

Another great thing about offline retail arbitrage is the ability to build and form relationships with the stores. If done and managed properly, these relationships can lead to you getting the "cream of the crop" so to speak, what I mean is you may find yourself able to access the store or inventory when others can't.

For example, you may have such a good relationship with the particular store that they call you when items you are looking for are available, or give you first run at them! A great relationship with a store is priceless. We will show you later on how to build and cultivate these relationships.

One of the most popular spots by far to retail arbitrage for a variety of goods is indeed Wal-mart.

Wal-mart has such a huge amount of items on clearance and sale at any given time that it makes for a great place to retail arbitrage. Even better, is that if you find a lot of one item for a good price, you often can get a manager and negotiate an even cheaper price! This does not always work, but it does more often than it does not!

Popular retail arbitrage items at Wal-mart include Bikes, Kids Powerwheel vehicles, electronics, and childrens toys!

A lot of times items can be found and sold for a premium of over 50%.

The most popular retail arbitrage opportunities are at clothing stores such as Victoria's secret. These name brand clothing stores have such a wide variety of not only clothes, but prices. These stores are constantly rotating and marking down inventory that the same item that sold for $30.00 yesterday is $12.00 today. That is how those stores work; you would be amazed what you can find once you learn their sale and markdown schedules. This is not limited to only Victoria Secret, but 90% of name brand clothing stores around.

One of the most expensive and popular retail arbitrage opportunities is women's handbags and purses.

For example, you can find Coach Handbags and purses at Coach Outlets or stores like Macys for drastically reduced prices compared to what they are actively selling on the internet. When it comes to high end handbags and purses, make sure you have all of your information right, the difference in a color or model can mean hundreds of dollars at times.

A Live Retail Arbitrage

Now that we know what retail arbitrage is, how it works, and have seen a few examples of it.

I am going to show you as close to a "live" retail arbitrage that does not even involve going to the store! Thanks to the internet, retail arbitrage can happen in seconds, opportunities are constantly becoming available, and once you know where to look, you will enjoy the profits and convenience!

Take a look at the listings below.

New! Abercrombie & Fitch Women's Mountain Fleece Jacket Size Medium, Large
Top Rated Plus
View similar active items | Sell one like this
FAST 'N FREE - Get it on or before Thu, Mar. 27

Mar-20 22 36

$74.90
Buy It Now
Free shipping

New! Abercrombie & Fitch Women's Mountain Fleece Jacket Size S, L
Top Rated Plus
View similar active items | Sell one like this
FAST 'N FREE - Get it on or before Thu, Mar. 27

Mar-20 22 29

$74.90
Buy It Now
Free shipping

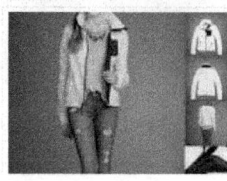

ABERCROMBIE & FITCH WOMEN mountain fleece JACKET SIZE M NWT white NEW 2013-2014
Top Rated Plus
View similar active items | Sell one like this
FAST 'N FREE - Get it on or before Thu, Mar. 27

Mar-19 20 18

$88.88
Best offer accepted
Free shipping

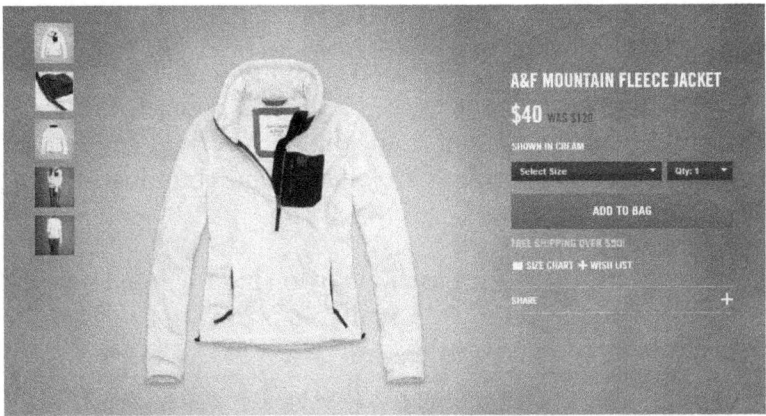

This is just one of many "active" examples, waiting to be found!

That price would yield a decent profit, however as the expression in business goes, you never want to leave money on the table. That same concept applies here let's look at a few ways to maximize our profits.

Now the next step is to get the most out of your arbitrage and sometimes it is as easy as entering a promo code, other times you have to be a bit more resourceful.

We will take the above example and continue to move forward with how to maximize your retail arbitrage profits.

Maximizing Your Retail Arbitrage Profits

If we were to purchase the above example today, we could use the promo code below for additional savings, this code was found easily on their homepage. However, sometimes promo and coupon codes are elusive and you must search for them.

9 times out of 10, the easiest way to find the most recent coupon or promo code available is to simply go to google.com and type in coupon [store name] or promo code [store name]. This will give you almost always exactly what you are looking for!

This coupon also offers free shipping too with purchases over $50.00.

UP TO 25% OFF YOUR PURCHASE + FREE SHIPPING OVER $50! PROMO CODE: 10711

This is a simple, yet effective retail arbitrage **found in less than 5 minutes** without ever leaving the computer, utilizing my resources available to me and not using the gas in my vehicle. This shows that ANYONE can do this; you just need to empower yourself and take action!

The goods will be conveniently shipped to me and all I have to do is make them available for someone else to purchase at a premium and that is what you call a successful retail arbitrage!

If my budget allowed it, I would want to purchase as many jackets as possible, but not before doing proper research such as the current market trend, as well as their sales volume on Ebay and Amazon.

Another thing to note is now that I am placing an order here, I would want to spend a little time trying to find a few more items to add to my order to also help maximize my profits. This is only if your budget allows it and also if it is not a current hot selling item in risk of going out of stock. If you find a hot item, do not waste your time browsing the store; be sure to check out as quickly as possible to avoid missing it.

Retail Arbitrage Calculations

This is a very basic formula that I use to calculate profitability of an item.

SP - PC - SC - MPF - AGP - Time - FBA = Profit

Where

SP - Selling Price (What you plan to sell it for)

SC - Shipping Cost (Can be found by finding the weight of the item once packaged and using a shipping calculator).

PC - Product Cost (Found on the store receipt)

Marketplace Fee - Depending on which marketplace/category within the marketplace you are selling on. (To get the marketplace fee take the Selling Price multiplied by the percentage fee, for example $100.00 x .15 (a 15% fee) would = $15.00 Marketplace fee.

AGP - Average Gas Price (Can be found by taking the day's gas costs divided by the total haul/items).

Time - If you are being compensated or want to bill for your time.

FBA - If you are utilizing FBA by Amazon, you will need to add these fees in every time you are calculating profitability

Profit - How much you will make after it's all said and done!

If after you do this calculation you are sitting with a 50% return or higher and are happy with that then you are ready to make your purchase!

Listing Your Product Online

Now depending on your research, you will most likely only be listing your item(s) on the most profitable marketplace.

Make sure you use a descriptive title and do not go overboard.

Use a 100% unique description that is not copied from anywhere. Make sure the description is exact and relevant to the item you are selling.

One of the most important factors in sales next to price and title is your pictures.

A proper listing will not only yield more exposure and thus more sales, but it can also help command a higher price over time when utilized correctly.

When it comes to listing your item, it is important to know which keywords to use. People rely on Terapeak for data when it comes to listing; I prefer to do it myself, with a mix of short and long-tail keywords.

Keyword Research

When you perform a search on Ebay, you will see below the search bar other search results that say related, typically as long as they are related to your item, they make great long-tail keywords, but keep in mind do not add/stuff keywords that are not related, it will get your listing removed!

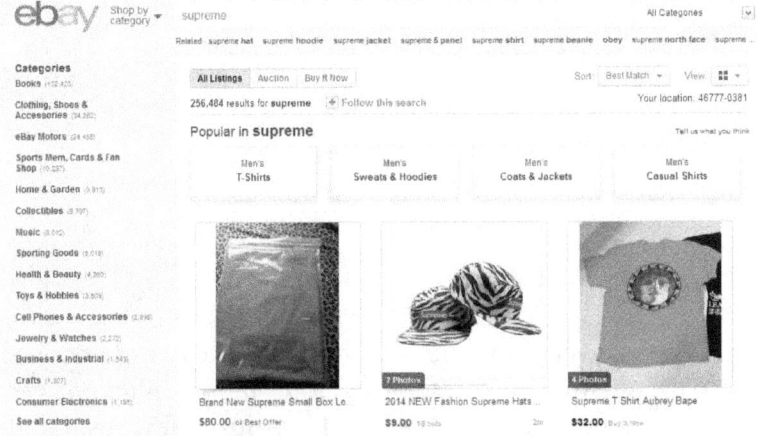

For example a main/short keyword would be, Supreme

A long tail keyword would be Supreme Mens Clothing, Supreme Hat, Supreme Hoodie, Supreme Jacket, etc..

You need to know which keywords people are looking for to help drive the most potential buyers to your listing.

This is a great way to do so, but I like to take it a step further and log into my AdWords account (adwords.google.com) an account is free and you do not have to actually advertise to use the keyword planner tool.

Once there, make sure you enter your term and select keyword ideas after searching. You should see something similar to the image below.

Your product or service

| supreme | | | | | Get ideas | Modify search |

Search terms		Avg. monthly searches [?]	Competition [?]	Suggested bid [?]	Ad impr. share [?]	Add to plan
supreme	⬐	165,000	Low	$0.44	0%	»

1 - 1 of 1 keywords ▾   <   >

Keyword (by relevance)		Avg. monthly searches [?]	Competition [?]	Suggested bid [?]	Ad impr. share [?]	Add to plan
supreme clothing	⬐	33,100	Low	$0.79	0%	»
supreme hats	⬐	14,800	Medium	$0.45	0%	»
supreme shoes	⬐	1,000	Low	$1.59	0%	»
supreme clothes	⬐	720	Low	$1.09	0%	»
supreme shirts	⬐	1,300	Medium	$0.83	0%	»

As you can see Supreme is a great main keyword and we also are seeing a few other good long-tails available if we have products related to them. This is just a few results of literally thousands!

When you gather your keywords you want to use, it's time to put them into a title! Make sure you try to rework your title at least 3 different times, you will be surprised at what you can do and the title is what makes the buyer click (besides the picture).

After you have your title together, take the same fundamentals and apply them to your description.

Your description is not as important as the title, price, or shipping, but it is very important.

A lot of buyers however, do not even read the description, they scan over it quickly after viewing the other information they deem more important.

Setting Your Price

This is arguably one of the most important parts of your listing.

If your price is too high, people won't want to buy your item.

If your price is too low, you are not making as much money and people may be suspicious of the quality.

It is always best at least for initial duration of your listing, to set your price as the lowest available, with free standard shipping, if possible.

If you are in a very competitive niche with multiple listings, some offering free shipping and some offering a lower price point and added shipping cost make 2 listings and compete on both ends.

Be sure to use a different title, description, and photo when doing this to avoid the "duplicate" listing policy.

By offering free shipping, you automatically get a boost in best match, and by offering free standard shipping, you are getting the fast and free boost in best match as well!

Now on top of the benefits of getting better best match placement, you are also now the lowest price point and most appealing listing!

When you set your price, (if you are offering free shipping) you need to keep in mind that you have built your domestic shipping costs into it.

So, when an international buyer is looking at your listing, make sure you take the added cost and subtract it out of the international shipping cost, this helps give them a break and simultaneously makes your listing more appealing to them.

You do not have to keep your item at the lowest price point, however for maximum salability it is a good idea to do so.

However, as your item gradually sells (if you have more than 1), you will notice it steadily moving up in best match and gaining popularity. As it does and as you sell, you can increase your price gradually. The higher you get in best match, the higher you can raise your price. Do not raise your price to a point that you become uncompetitive, it is important to find a good equilibrium when using the sale method or price method.

How Pictures Impact Your Listing

The best photos follow the below standards, set forth by Amazon.

They have spent millions researching consumer behavior and they have a pretty strong grasp of what works and what does not, especially when it comes to pictures.

Follow the below guidelines to get the best pictures for your listing every time!

• The image must be the cover art or a professional photograph of the product being sold. Drawings or illustrations of the product are not allowed.

• The image must not contain gratuitous or confusing additional objects.

• The image must be in focus, professionally lit and photographed or scanned, with realistic color, and smooth edges.

• Books, Music, and Video/DVD images should be the front cover art, and fill 100% of the image frame. Jewel cases, promotional stickers, and cellophane are not allowed.

• All other products should fill 85% or more of the image frame.

• The full product must be in frame.

• Backgrounds must be pure white (RGB 255,255,255).

• The image must not contain additional text, graphics, or inset images.

For additional other view images:

• The image must be of, or pertain to, the product being sold.

• The image must be in focus, professionally lit and photographed or scanned, with realistic color, and smooth edges.

• Other products or objects are allowed to help demonstrate the use or scale of product.

• The product and props should fill 85% or more of the image frame.

• Cropped or close-up images are allowed.

• Backgrounds and environments are allowed.

• Text and demonstrative graphics are allowed.

You can use websites like Picmonkey.com to get the most out of your photos and it's free!

Selling Worldwide

You have the option to sell within your country only, or offer your goods to everyone worldwide.

A lot of people just choose to sell their goods within their own country out of fear of being scammed.

While this is a great and safe practice, they are missing a very large amount of buyers.

EBay's main goal is to enable global trade and bring together buyers and sellers from around the world!

EBay recently implemented the global shipping center option for some products and categories, this is a great way for sellers to get the worldwide exposure they want without the risk of shipping internationally.

The issue with this is, a lot of potential buyers either do not use the GSC or it is not offered in their country.

It is best to offer all options, that way you are not alienating yourself from any potential buyers.

There are methods that can be used to help reduce risk and protect you from international scams.

For example when selling worldwide, only ship with a service that has delivery confirmation, for example USPS Priority mail, USPS Priority mail express, or Global Express Guarantee.

It is best to ship with USPS Priority Mail as it is the cheapest and most efficient for you and the buyer.

ALWAYS INSURE YOUR PACKAGES AND GET A RETURN RECEIPT IF POSSIBLE!

(This is all purchased at the post office if you printed your label online)

Both are essential to being able to protect yourself and the prices for the services should be built into your international shipping costs.

You never ship to any other address then the address that Paypal or Ebay tells you to on your transaction details page, if the buyer requests that, it is known as an unreasonable demand, report them to Ebay and cancel the transaction. By reporting them, you are helping to protect another seller who may not be as prepared as you in dealing with fraud.

Follow these steps and you will be protected from fraud in more ways than one!

USPS has started offering a new service with their first class international mail and some flat rates for E-Delcon delivery confirmation.

This service is only available to certain countries; however it is very smart to offer it. The best way to offer the service and insure your packages is to use the flat rate envelopes, padded flat rate envelopes, and small flat rate boxes. If you do not use these and just do the First Class Mail international, you are unable to insure the package, this could lead to issues since the delivery is slower with first class, the buyer might try to open a claim of non-delivery. You can always appeal a case once the item is delivered and get your money back, however it is just best not to go through this and use the envelopes as they get to the destination with the Priority mail speed, but have the first class price.

Here is a list of countries that you can currently use this service for.

Australia	Israel
Belgium	Italy
Brazil	Latvia
Canada	Lithuania
Croatia	Luxembourg
Denmark	Malaysia
Estonia	Malta
Finland	Netherlands
France	New Zealand
Germany	Portugal
Gibraltar	Singapore
Great Britain and Northern Ireland	Spain
Hungary	Switzerland

When printing your label, (use Ebay labels for the commercial discount), you need to make sure the country indeed is offering the service. If you see the E-USPS DELCON INTL, they are offering it.

Your postage cost

Postage cost:	--
E-USPS DELCON INTL™:	--
Total:	▬▬

☐ Display postage value on label

[Continue] [Cancel]

How to Keep Your Customers Coming Back Without Effort!

This is a no brainer really; you offer your customers an easy to redeem incentive.

For example, you offer your customers 1% cashback on their initial purchase for signing up with you to receive emails every 2 weeks. Then on all future purchases while the customer is enrolled they enjoy 1% cashback, you also email them every 2 weeks.

Now I know what you are thinking, this sounds like a lot of work, reaching out to clients, giving those refunds and adjustments, then making a list, and emailing them. You are right it **does sound** like a lot of work.

However, there is a great **free service** to EBay sellers called **Mystore Rewards**, that automates the entire process for you and I do mean the entire process.

MyStoreRewards is actually two powerful tools in one. First, it is an elegantly simple buyer reward program that quickly and easily tracks and rewards your loyal buyers when they buy from you. Second, it is a completely automated and eBay compliant opt-in email program. Best of all, it is free for all sellers.

How does MyStoreRewards work?

Sign-up takes just two minutes in the SMP Echo program. Once you sign-up, we will automatically place a few lines of HTML code within all your eBay listings. The image notifies all buyers to expect one invitation email inviting them to join your MyStoreRewards program. The HTML

code shows an image on your eBay listings.
Note: A 1% cash-back offer is the default value; you can set it at whatever percent you wish after you sign-up

This image is shown to your buyers before they buy. Since they will know they are getting cash-back, many will bid higher helping to actually increase your average-selling-prices! This simple image above starts the process by notifying your buyers they will get an invitation email to join your MyStoreRewards program when they purchase from you.

Only one invitation email is sent, promptly, and looks like this:

MySt☺reRewards
The simplest rewards program on earth.

Dear buyer,

Thank you for your recent purchase from **XXXXXXXX**. We received your payment of $80.60 on January 12, 2009. You automatically qualify to join our MyStoreRewards program where you can easily earn cash reward rebates on all your purchases (including this one!).

To receive a 1% cash reward rebate right away, and to earn automatic rebates on future purchases, please read and accept these rules by clicking the link below within 7 days of this email.

1. By clicking the link below you enroll in MyStoreRewards and will receive a 1% cash rebate of the amount shown above. To automatically earn future rebates when you purchase with us, always pay using the same registered email account: xxxxxx@hotmail.com. Your seller will send your reward via PayPal so your PayPal account must remain active and be capable of receiving payments to participate.
2. You will not incur any PayPal fees for receiving your rebates. Rebates are paid in the currency of the item purchased and cannot exceed 10.00 in the currency paid, in any 24 hour period. Any refunds for returned items will be reduced by the rebate amount rewarded to you.
3. By enrolling in MyStoreRewards, you agree to receive periodic emails from my account at www.MyStoreRewards.com. Your email is always kept confidential and you may opt-out of MyStoreRewards at any time. Review our Buyer Privacy Policy here. If you do opt-out of MyStoreRewards, you will no longer be eligible for future cash rewards.
4. MyStoreRewards is 100% free to my buyers like you. I may cancel the MyStoreReward program at any time.

Yes, I enroll. Please give my 1% MyStoreReward rebate.
OR
No thanks, I do not wish to enroll now or in the future.

It is all automated and free, nothing beats that. You may ask why they offer this, because whenever you make a sale, they make money as an EBay affiliate; however **you own the email list** and I will get into how to further profit from that shortly.

You can read their FAQ and learn more about what they do and why they do it.

Building Your Own Customer List

Building your own list is essential to your long term business. It can not only help you increase your profits by moving away from extra fees and hassles, but it can also give you a more direct relationship with your customers.

The **best option** is to carefully reach out to every customer you make a sale with on EBay or other online marketplaces that do not allow you to engage directly with customers outside their marketplaces.

How you do this is by first including either a business card, thank you letter, or small ad about your business with their order.

The next step is to take their email address and general purchase information from the PayPal transaction. Please note EBay does not allow you to get email addresses or engage in direct contact, which is why you are getting the information from your **PayPal transaction**. Make sure you record with their contact information, what they purchased, for how much, and the general transaction experience or note about them for future reference when reaching out or communicating it can be vital when dealing with a lot of customers.

You want to record most of this information at the beginning of the transaction before you ship the item! Remember to note the transaction experience after it is fully completed. A spreadsheet makes saving and recalling this information very easy.

Now when you ship the item, you typically automatically include a note to your buyer with the tracking and shipping information.

Please note: If you do not send a note with your shipping information it is time to start doing so. You need to include in the note, a positive message, and also how to subscribe to your store and add you to their favorite sellers. All of these links are easily made and available through EBay already.

You can first just copy the note that you would normally send and then email it directly to them from your registered contact email address that they made the payment too.

The other option is just to send two notes, one with their shipping information through Ebay and the other with the direct contact via Email.

Make sure you put in the note when making direct contact, that if they need help with anything else, to please do not hesitate to contact you. Also, highlight other products you have available that you think they may have an interest in and (optional) offer further incentive to purchase those products.

Invoicing Your Customers Directly

Now for invoicing your customer, you can use PayPal and their invoice tools, just click request money and create an invoice.

Once there you will have a fully customizable item lined invoice. You can add your business information, logo, and terms of sale. You can also customize a default template so all of these settings load automatically for you every time you create an invoice, both simple and efficient.

Creating an invoice is as simple as filling in the details and then clicking send!

Scaling Your Email List

Now when it comes to building a more mass engaged list, I would recommend a service like Mailchimp.

Mailchimp allows you to use their services free until you reach 2,000 subscribers and you can send up to 12,000 emails a month with their forever free plan!

Once you have them in your list, you can email them at your leisure when you feel you have something engaging and informative to let them know about, you are not put on a bi-weekly limit like Mystore rewards has, they will be still automatically emailed through that free service as long as they are enrolled and you are still utilizing it.

Hitting the 2,000 subscriber limit is a milestone for any business and signifies not only the growth, but the continuing success of your business. This should be a major goal for you and your business if it is not already.

The great thing about building your list is that it ultimately ends up with the customer engaging one on one with you without a middleman or contact intermediary.

This means you are engaging repeat customers on a direct basis. You are not only saving fees and making more profit, but providing the customer with a better experience, which will lead to more business!

Establishing and Cultivating Retail Relationships

Once you are comfortable buying, it is time to work on establishing your retail relationships with the store managers at the places you frequent.

Often times, it pays to talk to these managers, as most of the time they get a bonus for a certain amount of goods sold or units moved. However, you can always make due by dealing with sales associates or assistant managers as well, because typically they get a bonus, although it is not as much as the store managers get usually.

Before you talk to anyone, make sure you look either online or in their store for their policies regarding quantities of items purchased.

Often times, they may have quantity limits imposed, however a lot of times store managers do not even limit quantities, because they are getting the bonus from you buying.

Once you are familiar with the stores policies and how they work, talk to the store manager and ask them their markdown or sale schedule.

Once you have that information, proceed to talk with them and ask them if it would be alright to leave your number and they call you whenever they have [product name] in stock.

This usually is not an issue, but sometimes they do not call, and it is best to follow up with a call in a week or so (or whenever your budget allows), and see if they have the item(s) you wanted them to call you about in stock.

By you doing a follow up call like this, it will establish two things to the store manager.

1. You are an active buyer who is always looking for this item(s).

2. It is ok to call or text message you.

Retail relationships can be a great addition to your retail arbitrage; however they are not required for success.

Building Your Own E-commerce Store (Outside of EBay)

You have learned Retail Arbitrage; you have successfully started growing your business and contacts. You are on your way to building up your email lists, and are direct invoicing some repeat customers.

Now you are ready to take it to the next step. You are ready to build your own E-commerce Website.

Securing a Domain and Hosting Provider

First step is to secure a reliable domain and hosting provider; I used to use Godaddy, but have recently moved to Digital Ocean. You can use my referral link and get $10.00 free to start. If you decide to use Digital Ocean, you will need to most likely outsource to a developer to get going.

This tutorial is set up for Godaddy.

Next step is to brainstorm your domain name and begin searching for it.

Over 1,000 websites are created a day, so it can get very competitive when trying to find the right domain name.

However, if you are lucky it will be available, remember do not just make up any name, put thought behind the **process** and **brand** you are creating!

The website domain name you pick will ultimately hopefully represent your brand and vision.

After a lot of thought and trying different domain names, you will have your **perfect domain name**.

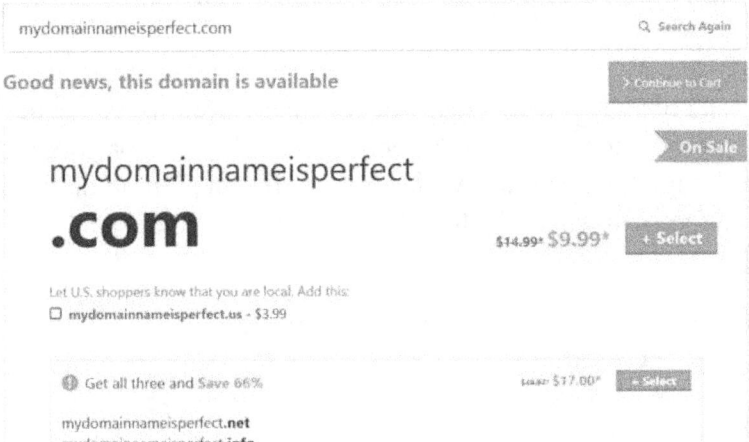

From there, get a coupon and cash back for whatever domain provider you decided on and check out!

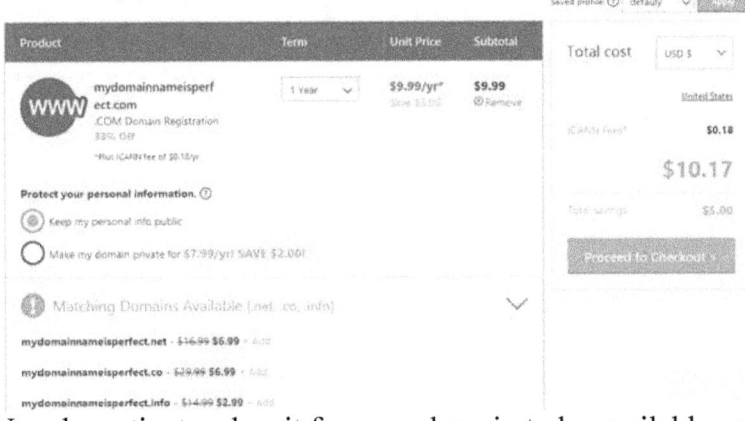

Now be patient and wait for your domain to be available on your account (typically within the hour).

Selecting Your Hosting Plan

The next step is to secure your web hosting; the process is pretty much the same. Select what works best for you; the budget plan should work for now. If you plan on having more than one website in the very near future, select your plan accordingly.

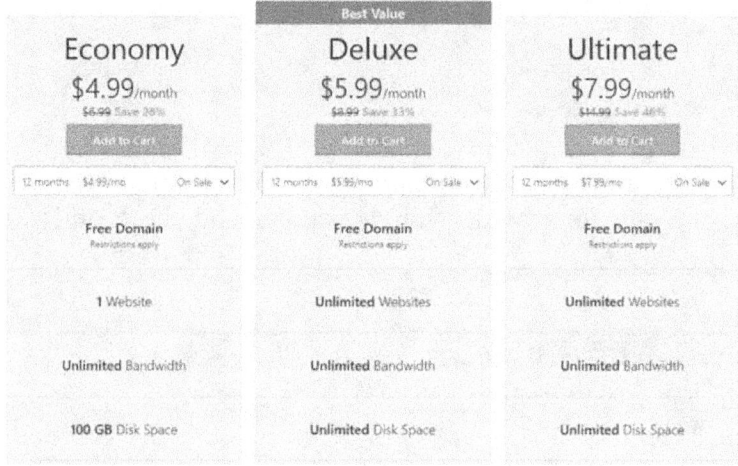

Configuring Your Web Hosting and Domain

Now once your web hosting and domain name is set up, it is time to put your domain name with your hosting.

This will be shown through Godaddy just as the above examples were.

Click Web Hosting, follow the instructions, and set up your new web hosting product so you can launch it.

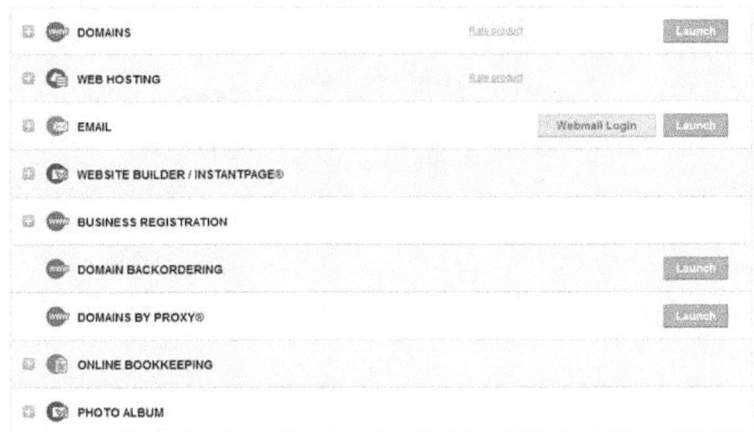

After that is done, launch it. After it loads, you will be on your dashboard screen for your web hosting.

You will see a basic screenshot of everything at a glance

Click where it says hosted domains.

Account Snapshot

Billing   Ultimate Secure

FTP Users

Applications

Databases

Hosted Domains   Domains

Email   Accounts

Bandwidth

Disk Space

You will be redirected to the hosting control center, which
shows all the domains currently on this hosting plan. You
should have 0, but if you are just using this for reference
then you may see some available on there.

Click Add Domain

Add Domain

A window will appear for you to add your domain and folder. Type the first 3 letters of your domain and it will come up below and select it from the list. The next step is very important, you will make its folder, I recommend using something easy as it is CASE SENSITIVE, so A and a are not the same!

Add Domain

- Domain
  Bulk

Adding a domain to this hosting account lets visitors access your content through a new URL. Deluxe and Premium plans can point an added domain to any new or existing subdirectory or nested subdirectory. To point this domain to the root ("/"), leave the default Folder setting. Economy plans can point to the root, only.

Domain: Folder:

[   ]   / [   ]   Browse...

OK   Cancel

After you choose your folder name hit OK. Make sure you write down or save your folder name, you will need it later!

You have successfully added your first domain to your hosting!

Now if everything goes alright on your hosts end, you should see it added within the next 1-24 hours.

Once your domain is added we will go back and launch our web hosting again.

Installing and Configuring WordPress

Log into Godaddy, select your web hosting and click Launch.

Once there, you will be back at your dashboard, be sure to click the hosted domains tab, and be sure that your domain is indeed added.

You will see under status it will say setup or setup primary, which means it's ready to go!

Navigate back to your dashboard. We are going to be using WordPress to make your first E-commerce website, it is by far the easiest to use and utilize for beginners and pros alike!

You will also see this below the snapshots. Click WordPress

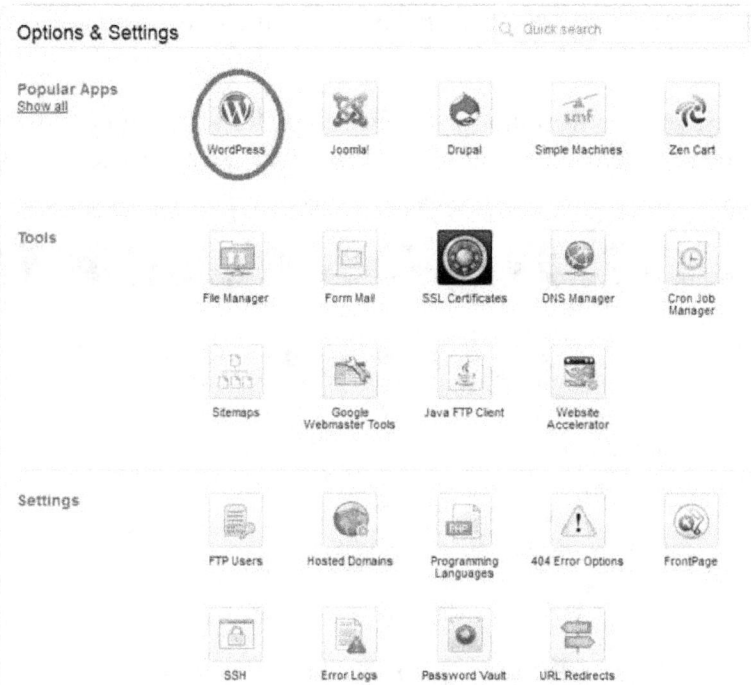

The following screen will appear.

Make sure you put in your domain name and the directory you original saved your domain name to on your web hosting!

Save the information somewhere safe, you will need it later! Not only that, but you do want to know how to access your website.

After you filled out all the details required, select OK.

While WordPress installs, utilize your time to find a WordPress theme and a few plugins to start off.

First we want to get the basic plug-ins we will need to successfully run our E-commerce website.

Plugins and Themes Needed

Download all of these zip files and place them in a folder you will remember.

DO NOT UNZIP the files, they will be uploaded zipped!

Woocommerce

XML Sitemap

Scroll to Top

Ultimate TinyMCE

W3 Total Cache

Next we want to get our theme for our website, it has to be woo commerce compatible, I recommend Elegant Themes, however if you are going for free, then go here and pick one of the available themes.

WooThemes

Save it in the same folder as the plugins.

Hopefully, by now WordPress is fully installed on your website and you have received an email telling you how to log in with a link. Click the link and bookmark it, enter in your login information and login.

You will be redirected to your admin dashboard for your website!

Once there on your left sidebar is a bunch of different tabs, which can be overwhelming at first, but you will learn how to successfully navigate your admin panel in no time!

Wordpress Dashboard – Clear Default Posts and Page

You will not be seeing the WooCommerce or Products tab yet, as you still have to upload your plugins.

First things first, click posts and delete the general post that says Hello World. This is done by hovering below the title and selecting trash, don't forget to empty your trash!

After that, click pages, and delete the sample page.

Installing Plugins

From there, you will then hover over the plugins tab and select add new.

Click Upload

Click Browse and upload a plugin, (you can only upload one at a time) after successfully uploading it, you will be redirect to a screen, be sure to click activate this plugin; otherwise it will not be active.

Do this until you have uploaded all of your plugins and successfully activated them; remember this is not where you upload your new theme at!

Install a WooCommerce Compatible Theme

Now that you have successfully installed and activated your plugins, you are ready to go ahead and upload your woocommerce compatible theme you selected!

Click on appearance or hover over it to open the secondary menu.

Click Themes

You will see the following, plus your current default theme.

Themes ❹   Add New   Search installed themes...

Click **Add New**

Just as you did with the plugins, you will do the same here.

Click Upload

Install Themes

Search | Upload | Featured | Newest | Recently Updated

Search for themes by keyword.

| | Search |

Click Browse and add the theme!

Install Themes

Search | **Upload** | Featured | Newest | Recently Updated

Install a theme in .zip format

If you have a theme in a .zip format, you may install it by uploading it here.

| Browse... | No file selected. | Install Now |

Upon successful completion you will be redirected to a similar page like the plugins and make sure you click activate this theme!

Setting Up Your WooCommerce Cart

Navigate to the WooCommerce part of your dashboard and select settings.

Begin filling in your store information.

Click each tab up at the top and fill in the information.

Now when you reach Checkout it is time to add your Paypal information.

General	Products	Tax	**Checkout**	Shipping	Accounts	Emails

Checkout Options | PayPal | BACS | Cheque | Cash on Delivery | Mijireh Checkout | CoinPayments.net

Checkout Process

Coupons ☑ Enable the use of coupons

Coupons can be applied from the cart and checkout pages.

Checkout ☑ Enable guest checkout

Allows customers to checkout without creating an account.

☐ Force secure checkout

Force SSL (HTTPS) on the checkout pages (an SSL Certificate is required).

Checkout Pages

These pages need to be set so that WooCommerce knows where to send users to checkout.

Cart Page ⑦ | Cart   × ▾ |

Checkout Page ⑦ | Checkout   × ▾ |

Click PayPal

The following page will appear.

Enable/Disable	☑ Enable PayPal standard
Title	PayPal
Description	Pay via PayPal; you can pay with your credit card or debit card if you don't have a PayPal account
	This controls the description which the user sees during checkout.
PayPal Email	
Receiver Email	
PayPal Identity Token	Optional
Invoice Prefix	SWW-
Payment Action	Capture ▾
Submission method	☐ Use form submission method. *Enable this to post order data to PayPal via a form instead of using a redirect/query string.*
Page Style	Optional
Shipping options	
Shipping details	☑ Send shipping details to PayPal instead of billing. *PayPal allows us to send 1 address. If you are using PayPal for shipping labels you may prefer to send the shipping address rather than billing.*

Fill in the details. Then click save.

Next click the shipping tab. It is best to just use free shipping and build the costs into your merchandise prices.

However, there are a variety of options and customizations that you can make later on down the road.

Now that we have set up every aspect of our cart, we are ready to add our products!

Adding Products to Your Website

Navigate to your wordpress admin panel.
(http://[mywebsite.com]/wp-admin)

Important, if you plan on having categories, be sure to add categories first. To do this, hover over the products tab and select categories.

Product categories for your store can be managed here. To change the order of categories on the front-end you can drag and drop to sort them. To see more categories listed click the "screen options" link at the top of the page.

Add New Product Category

Name

The name is how it appears on your site.

Slug

The "slug" is the URL-friendly version of the name. It is usually all lowercase and contains only letters, numbers, and hyphens.

Parent

None ⌄

Description

All you have to do is enter in the name of the category and click add, it will fill in the rest.

After you add your categories, hover to the products tab below WooCommerce and select add product.

You will see the following screen.

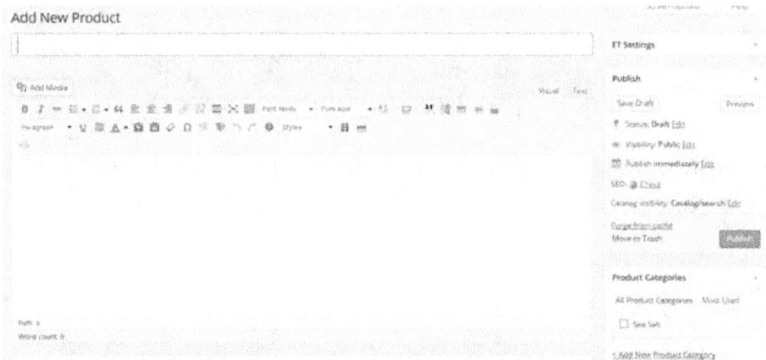

The name of your product goes up top.

The description of your product goes below.

Note your product categories for you to select from, as well as the ability to preview your product posting as you work on it.

Once you add this information, the next step is to add the product featured image.

The product image tab is your featured image, so you upload the main picture to it.

The other is the product gallery for any additional photos.

You use the product tags to add descriptive tags about you item such as blue t shirt, or the brand.

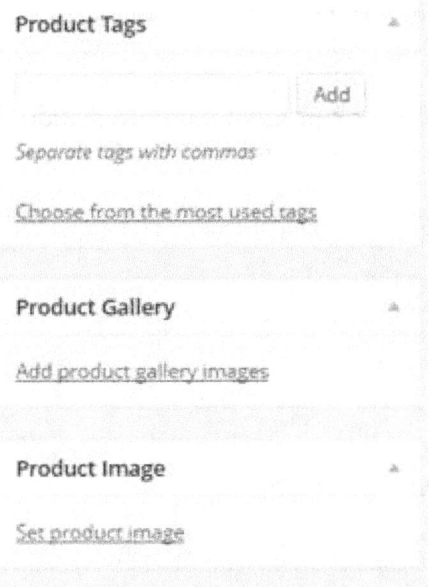

After that it is time to configure your products price and quantity.

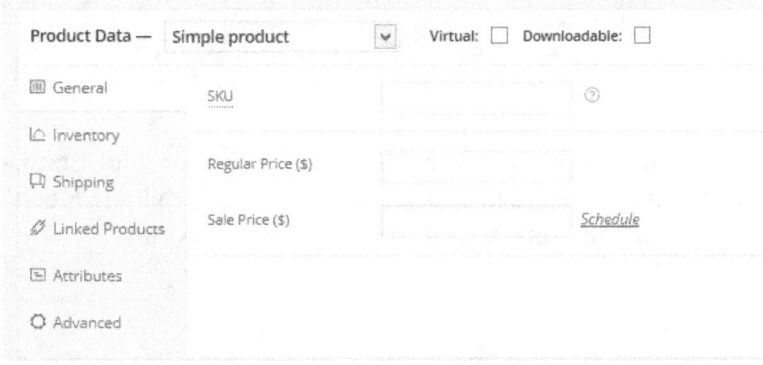

Select simple product.

Enter the regular price and sale price, or just the regular price if you want.

Click the inventory tab, set your inventory. Do the same for shipping if you plan to charge for it.

You can also link products; it will also do that for you automatically.

From there, scroll up and click Publish.

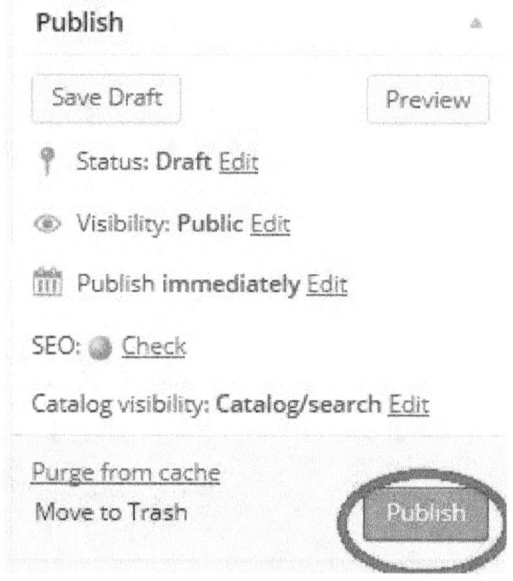

Congratulations, you have successfully created your first E-commerce website and launched your first product! **Keep taking action and growing your business!**

50 Places to Perform a Retail Arbitrage

Here is a list of 50 locations where you can successfully perform a Retail Arbitrage, no matter what your experience is! It's time to take action now! Find a store(s) you feel comfortable with and begin your research!

1. The Children's Place

2. Osh Kosh B'Gosh

3. Carter's

4. Gymboree

5. Victoria Secret

6. Wal-mart

7. Adidas

8. Famous Footwear

9. Finish Line

10. Tommy Hilfiger

11. Macys

12. Marshalls

13. Supreme

14. Coach

15. Ralph Lauren

16. Gap

17. Abercrombie

18. Kohls

19. JC Pennys

20. Armani

21. Meijer

22. Guess

23. Kenneth Cole

24. Old Navy

25. Gucci

26. American Eagle

27. Burberry

28. Ecko

29. Vera Bradley

30. Nike

31. North Face

32. Under Armour

33. Puma

34. Eddie Bauer

35. Reebok

36. Prada

37. K Swiss

38. Lane Bryant

39. Lacoste

40. Affliction

41. TJ Maxx

42. Home Depot

43. Lowes

44. Menards

45. CVS

46. Wal-greens

47. Nike

48. Target

49. Claires

50. The Buckle

And of course at any outlet store!

What I Started With

Thank you for purchasing my book. I hope you found it to be informative and helpful. This book is the culmination of my experience learned, not taught. If I would have been given this information when I first started, I would have saved easily 5 years. Best of luck and now it is on you to get started!

Questions? Contact me at info@retailarbitrage.org

www.ingramcontent.com/pod-product-compliance
Lightning Source LLC
Chambersburg PA
CBHW070842180526
45168CB00002B/927